Cat-nip for the Soul:
A Mandala Coloring Book

By Debbie Huber
Honeybee Publishing

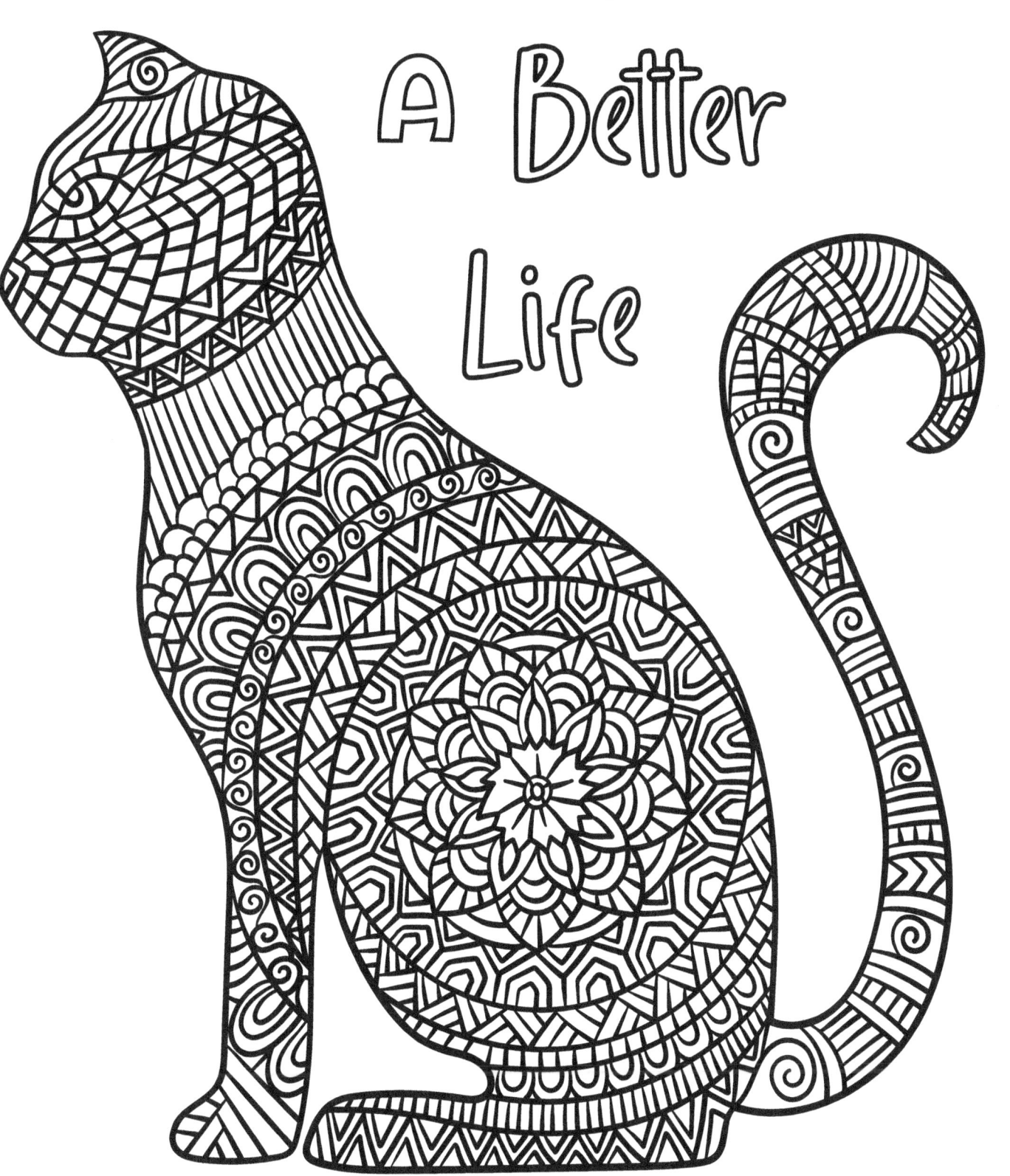

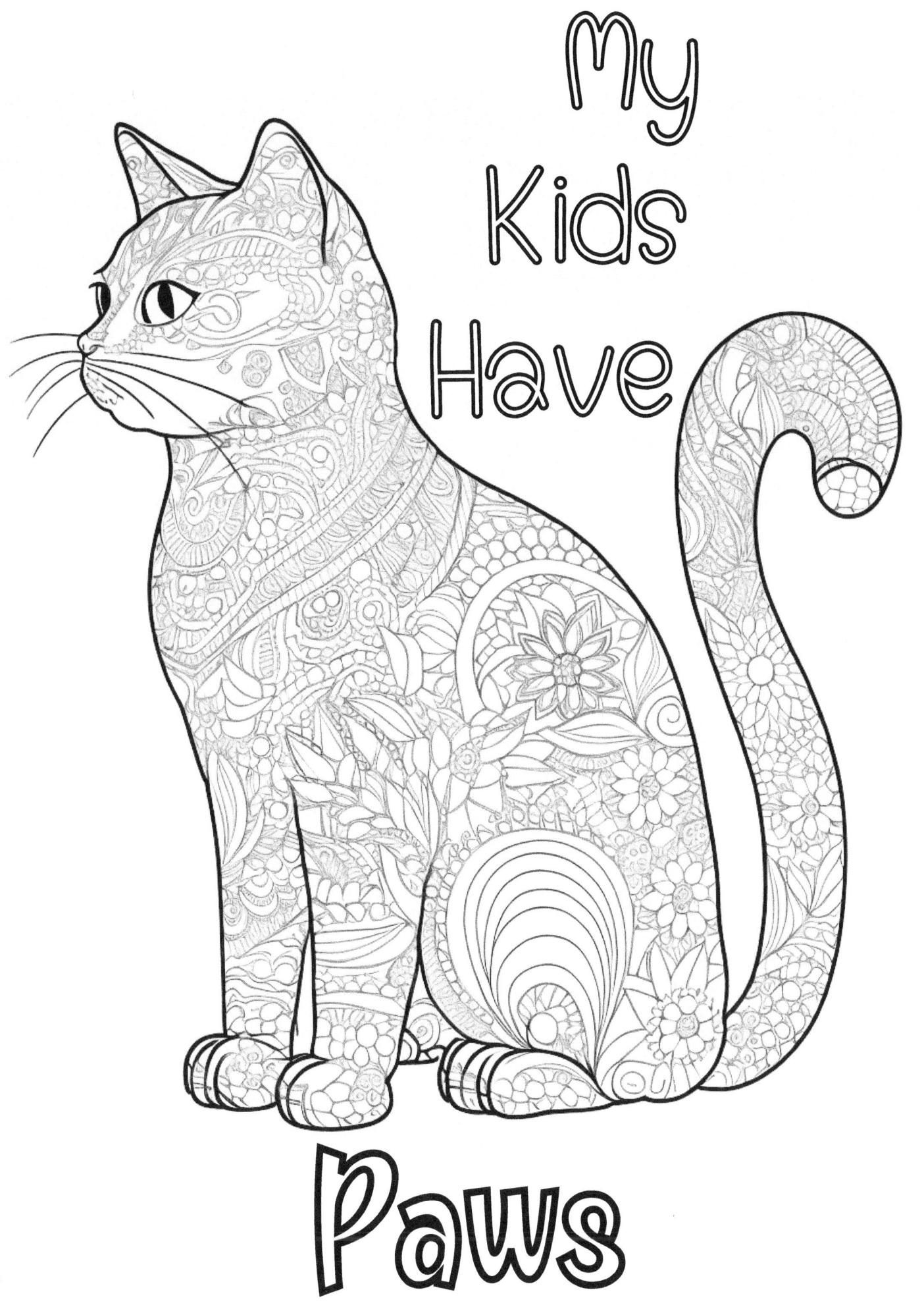

My
Kids
Have

Paws

I only talk

To Cat People

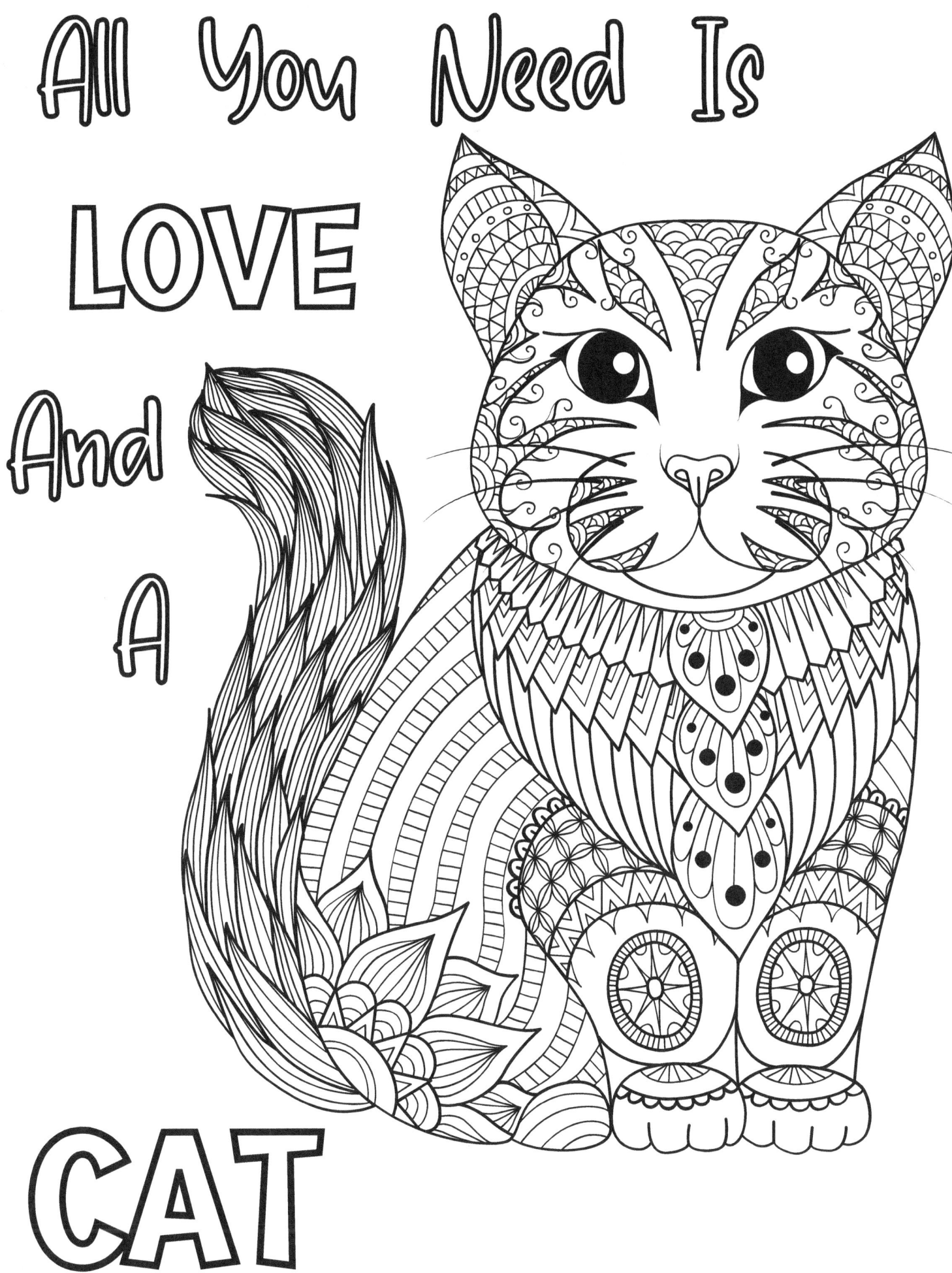

All You Need Is LOVE And A CAT

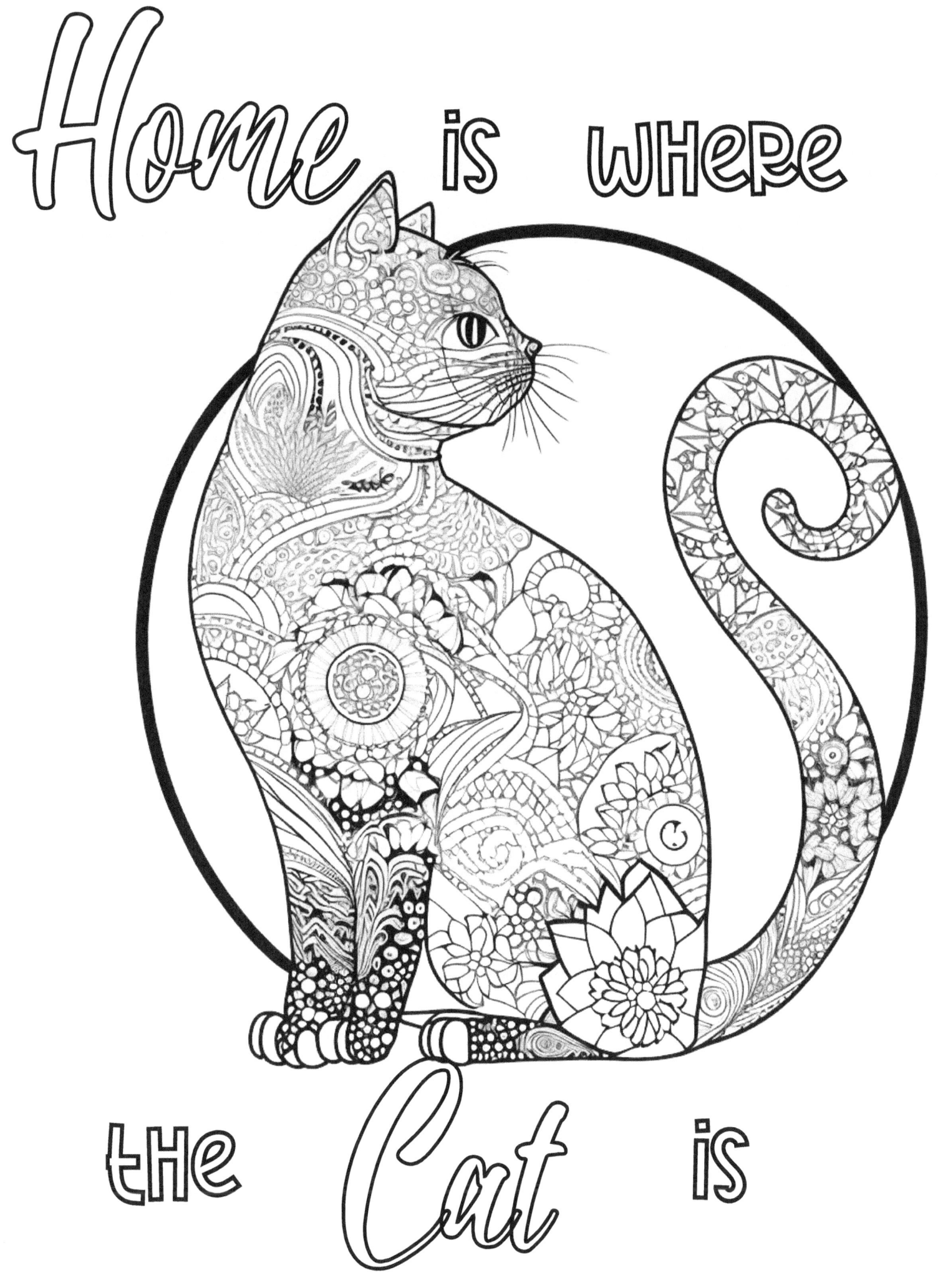

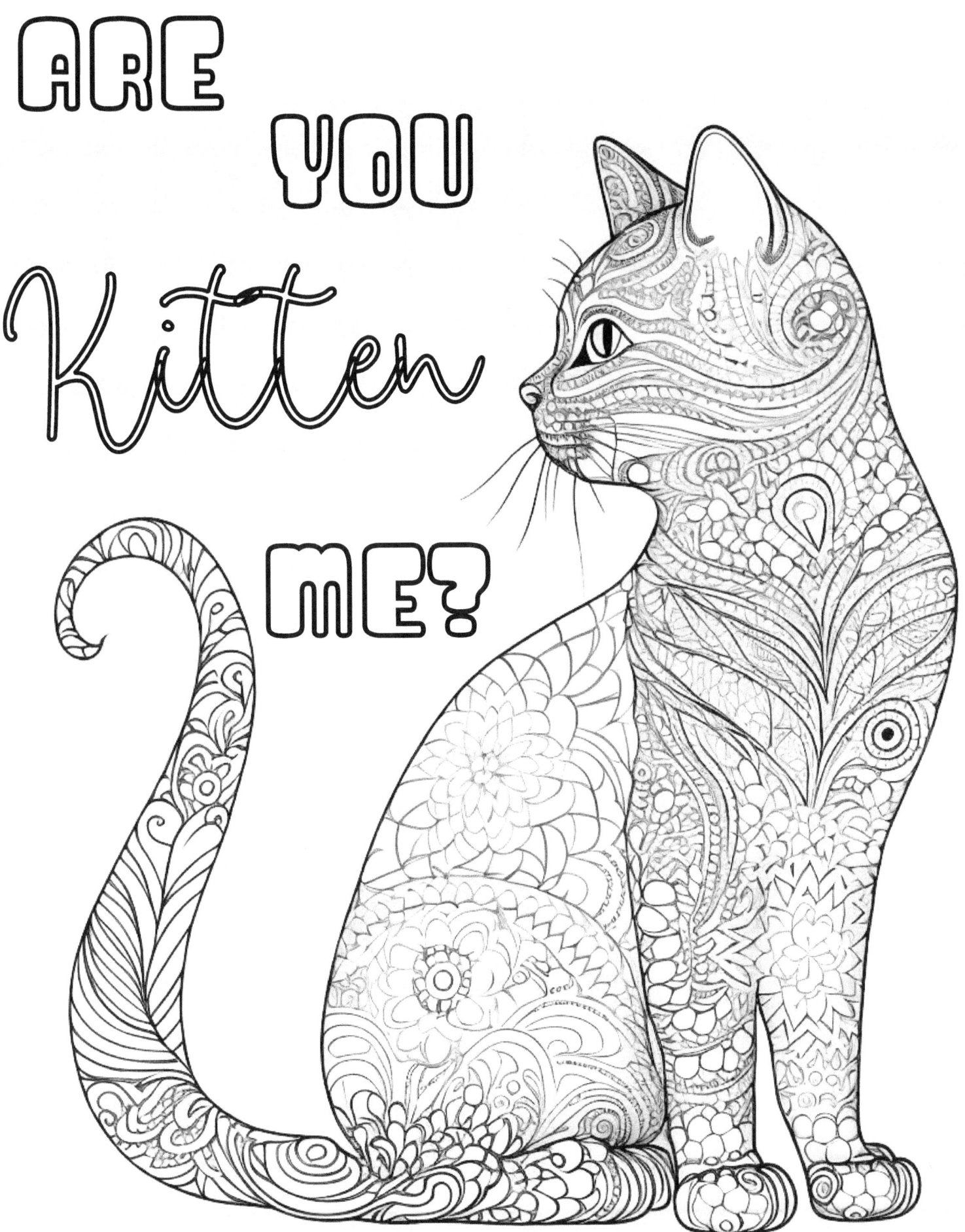

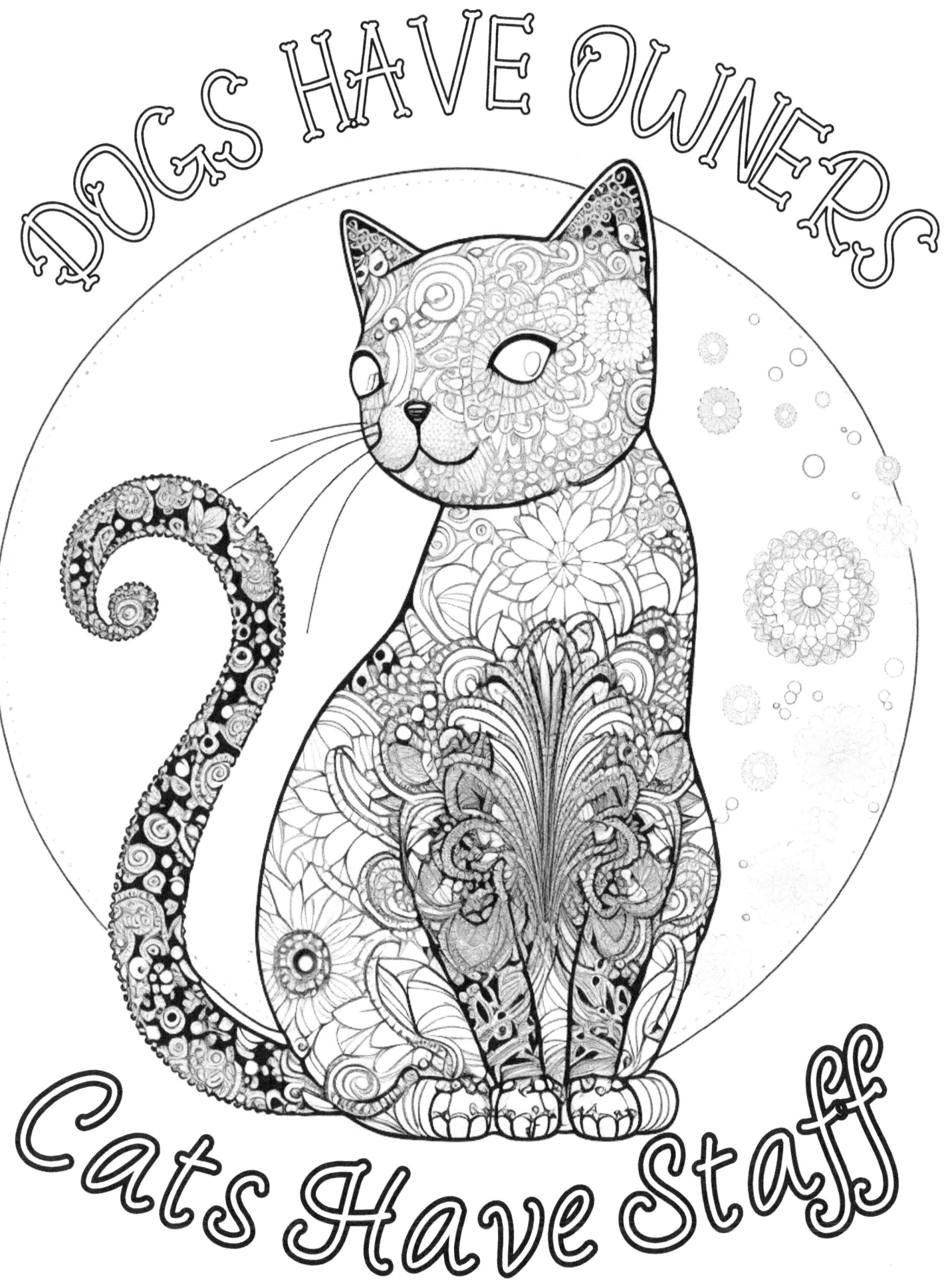

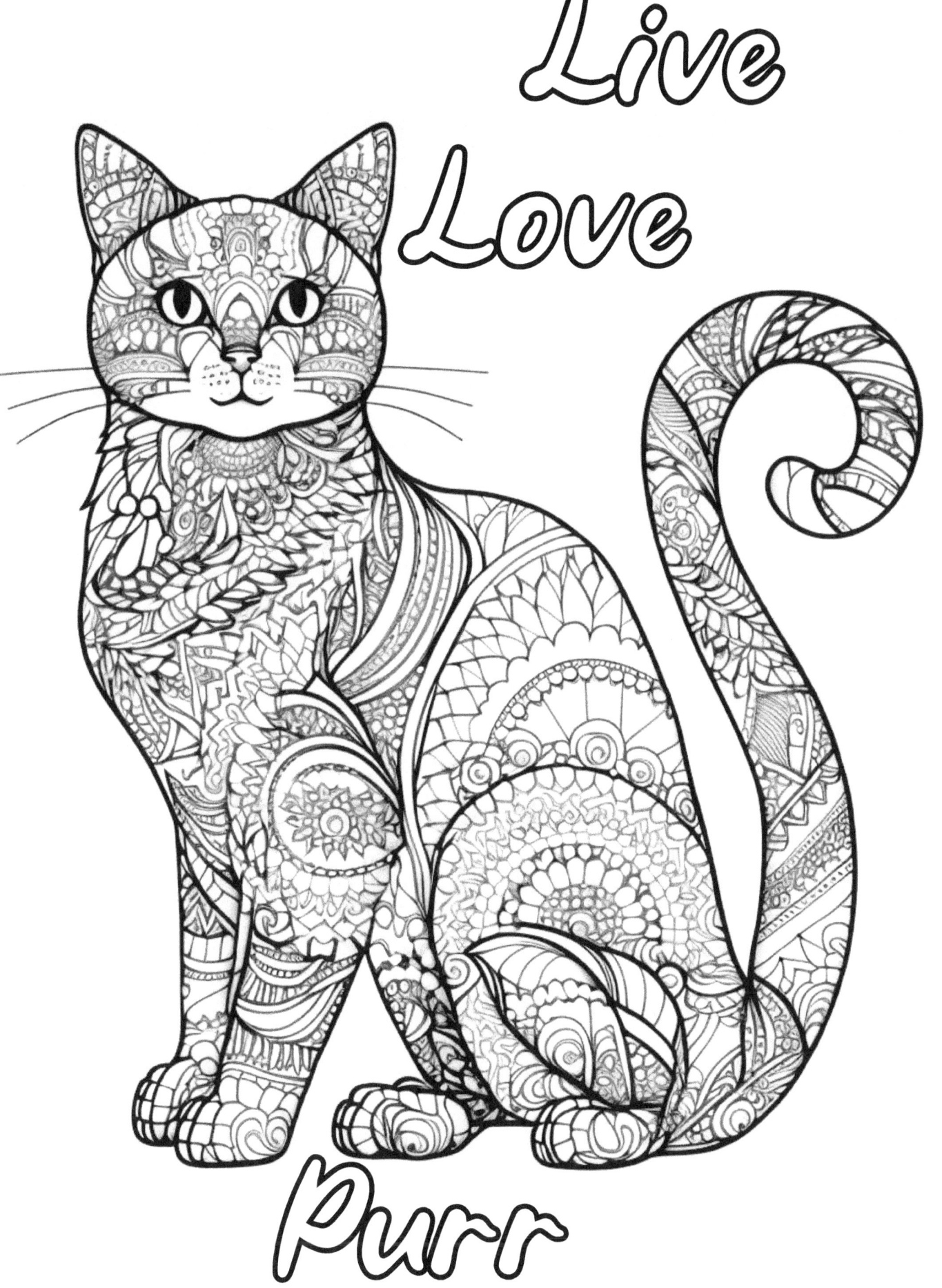

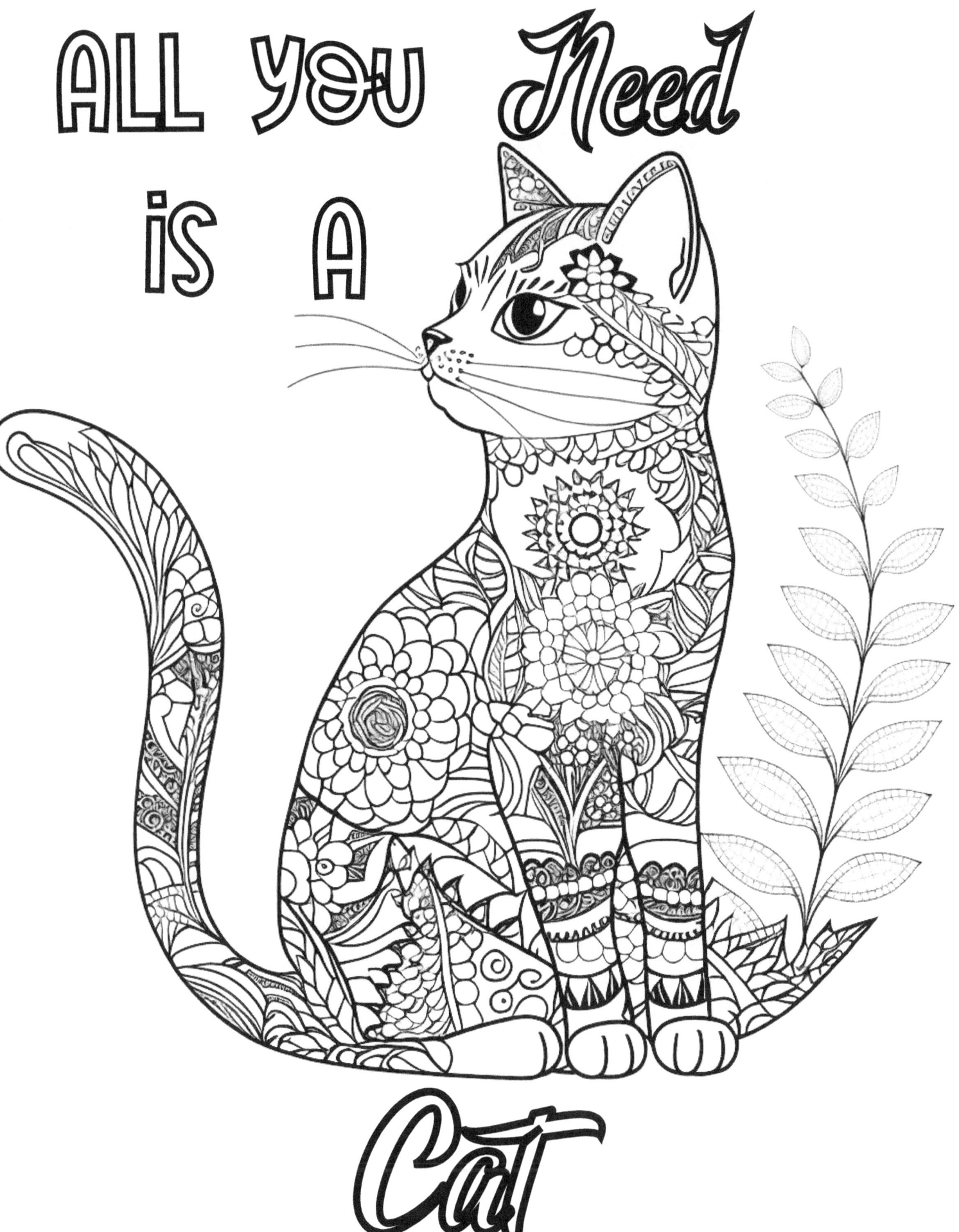

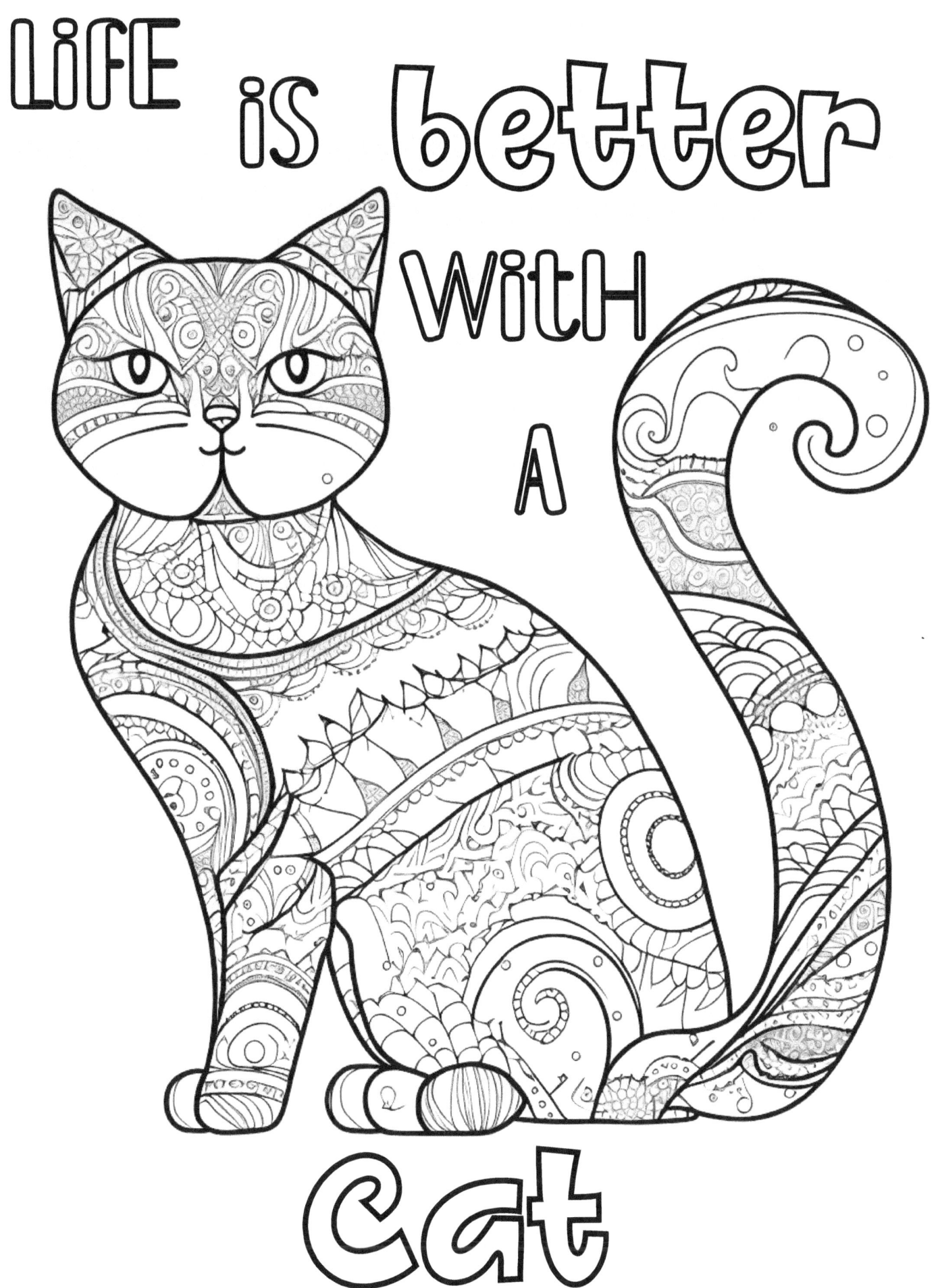

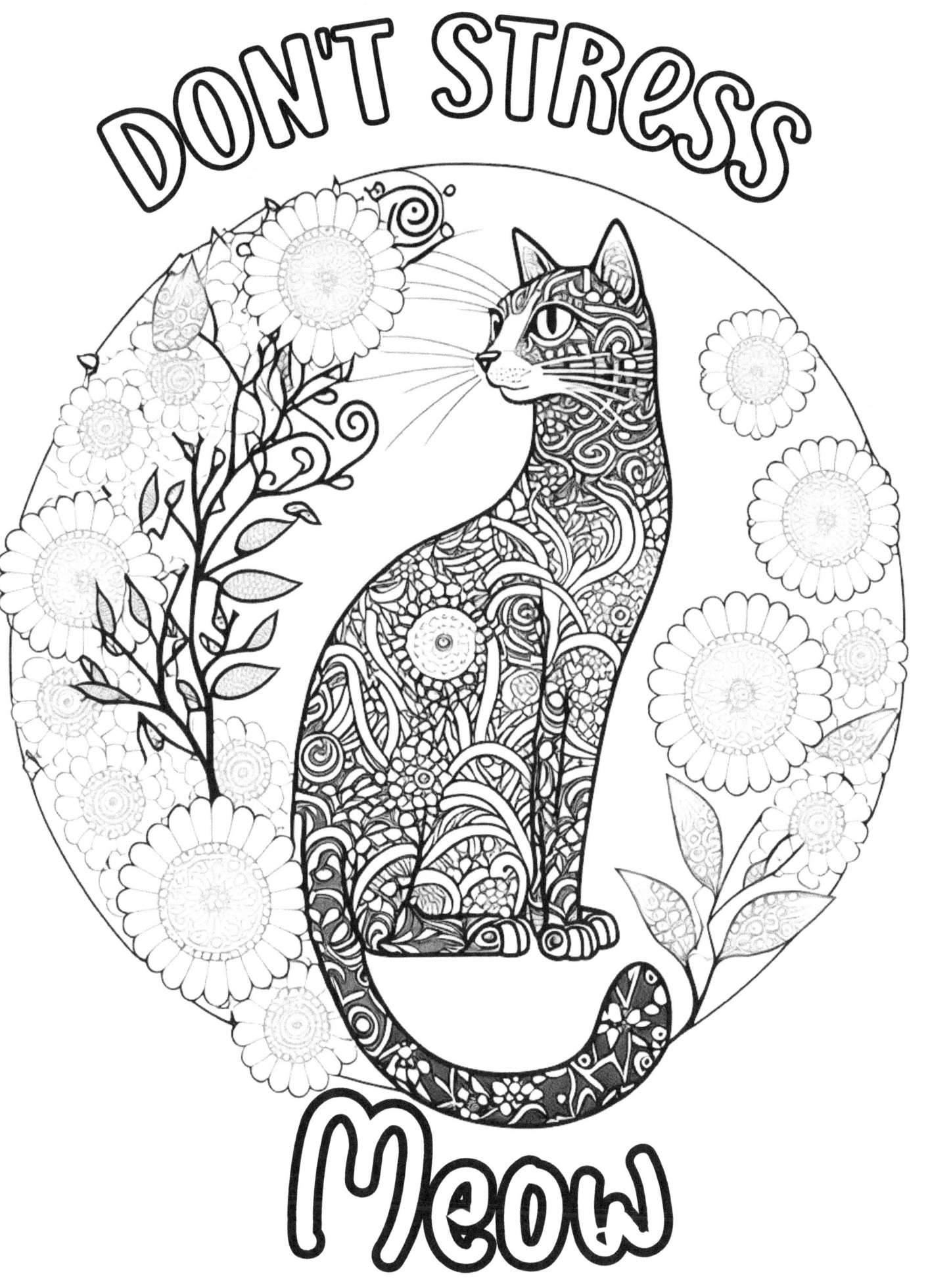

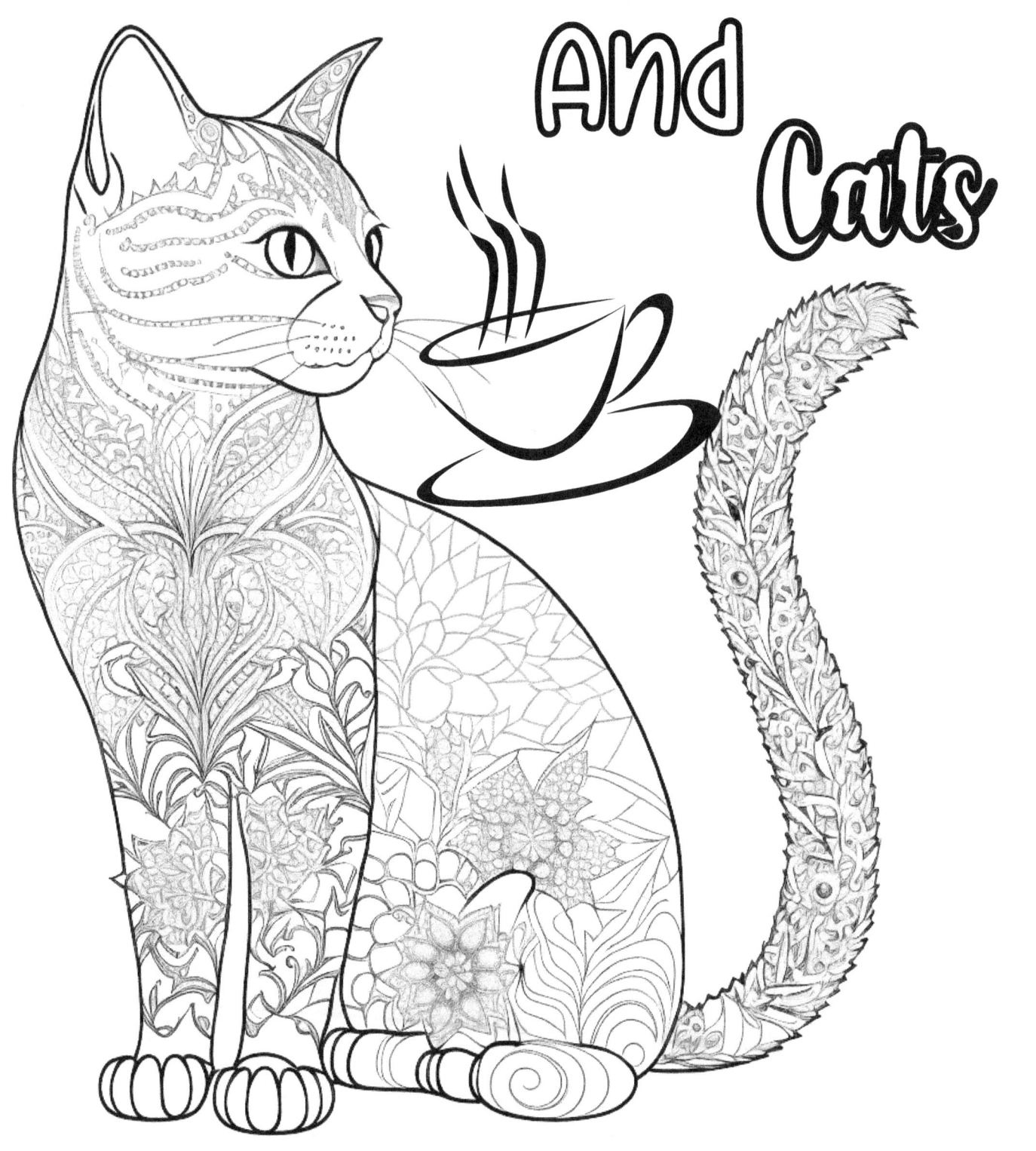

Blessed and Cat Obsessed

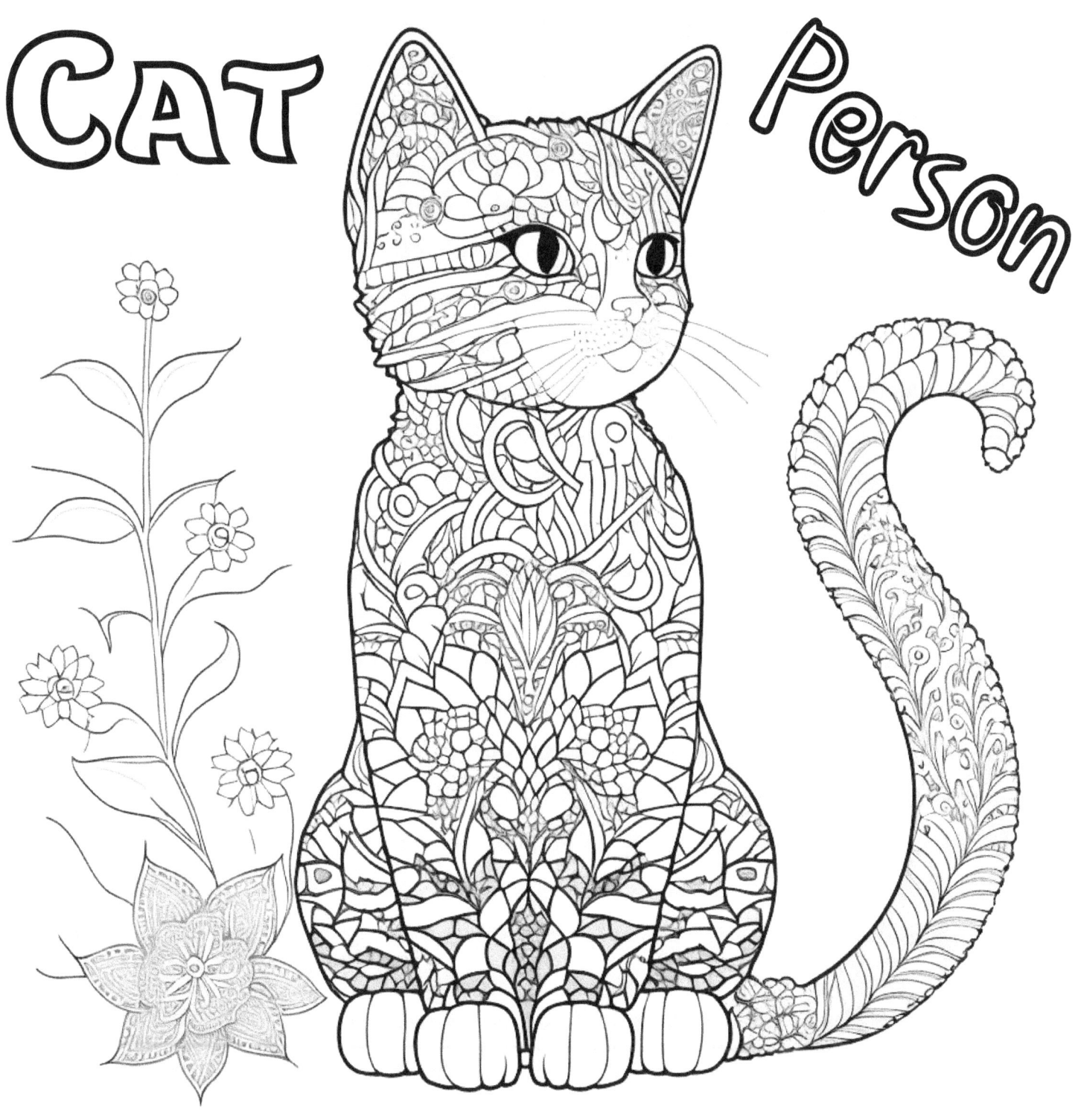

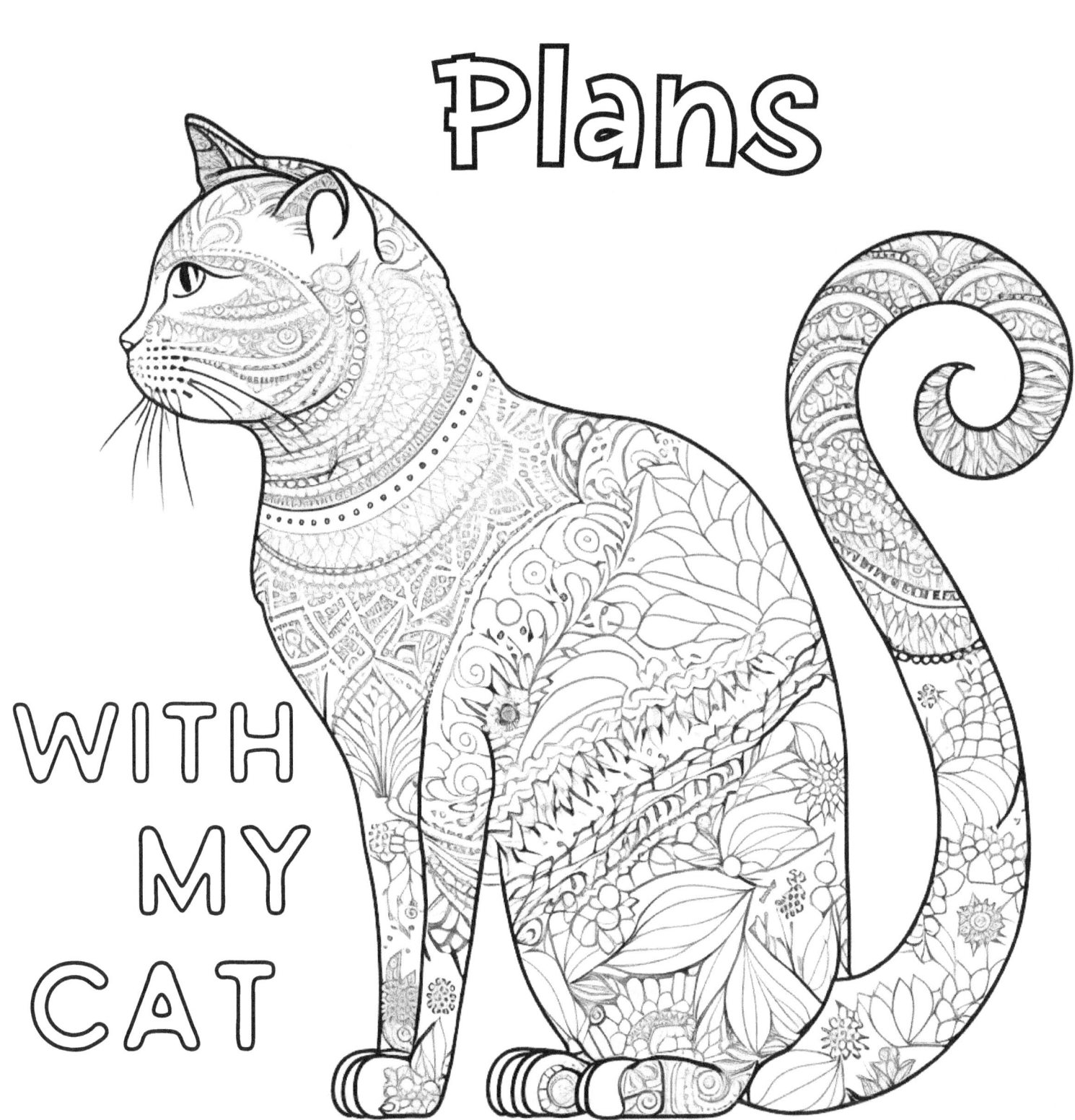

Love　　　　Me

LOVE　　MY　　CAT

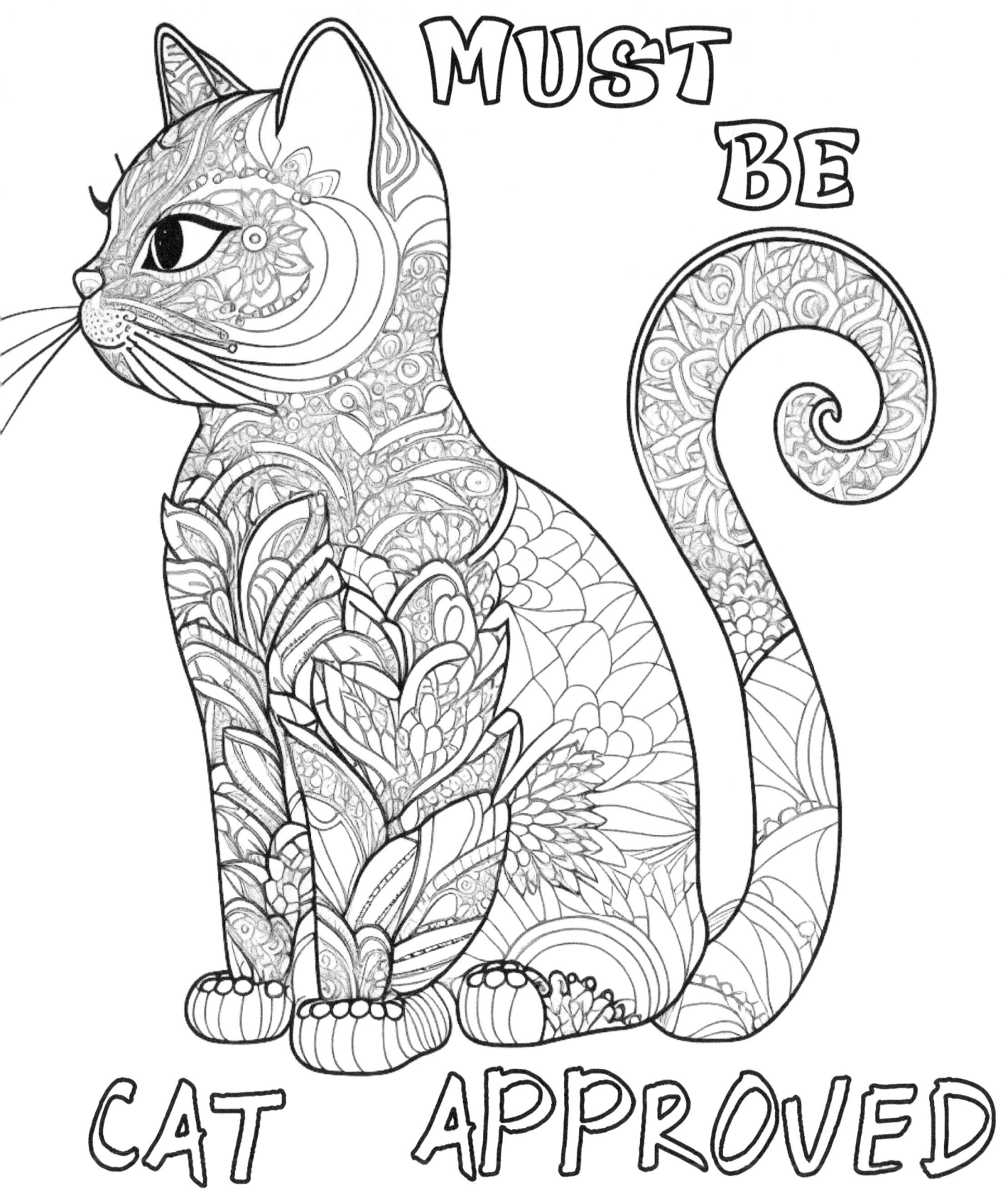

Cats Are My

Favorite People

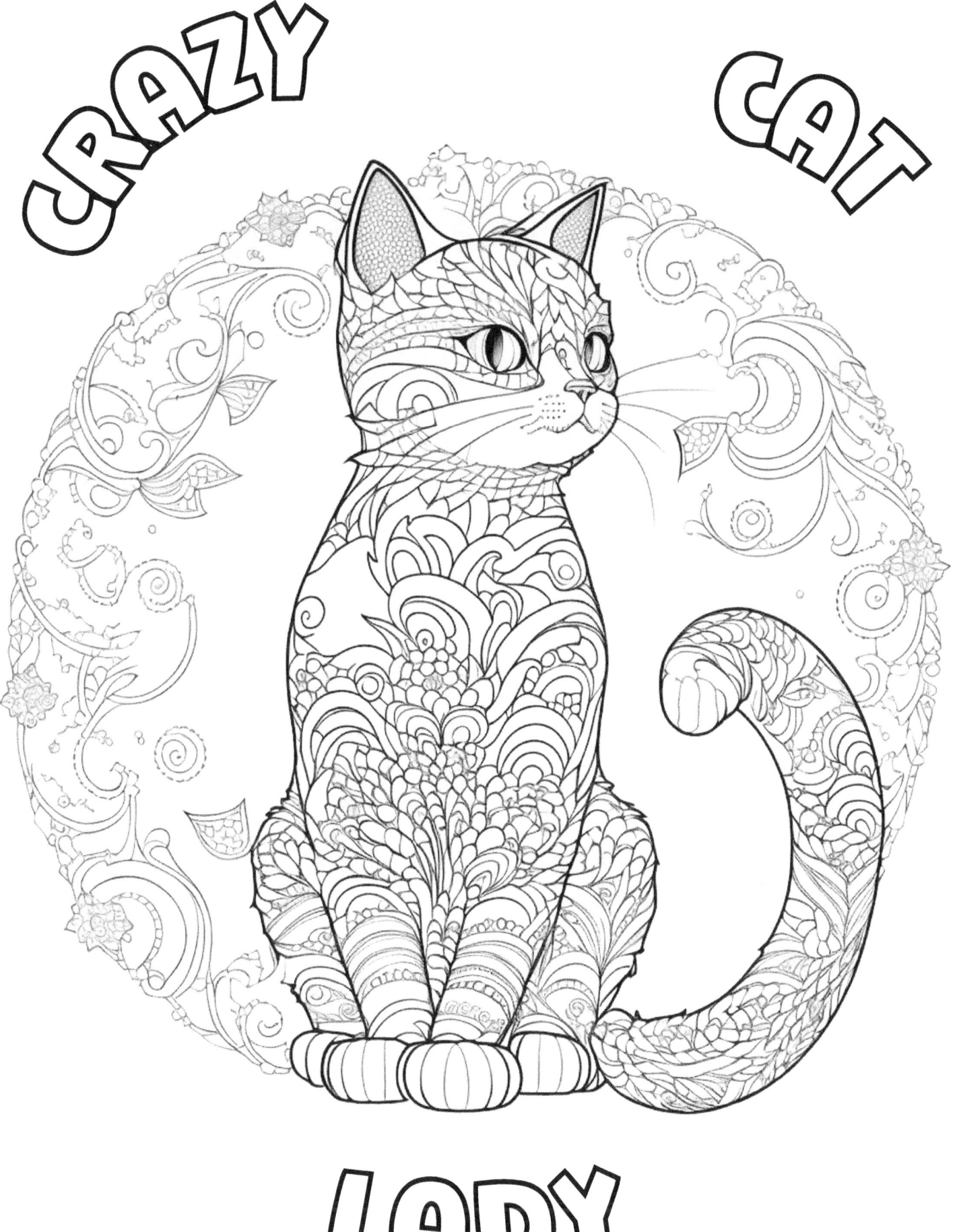

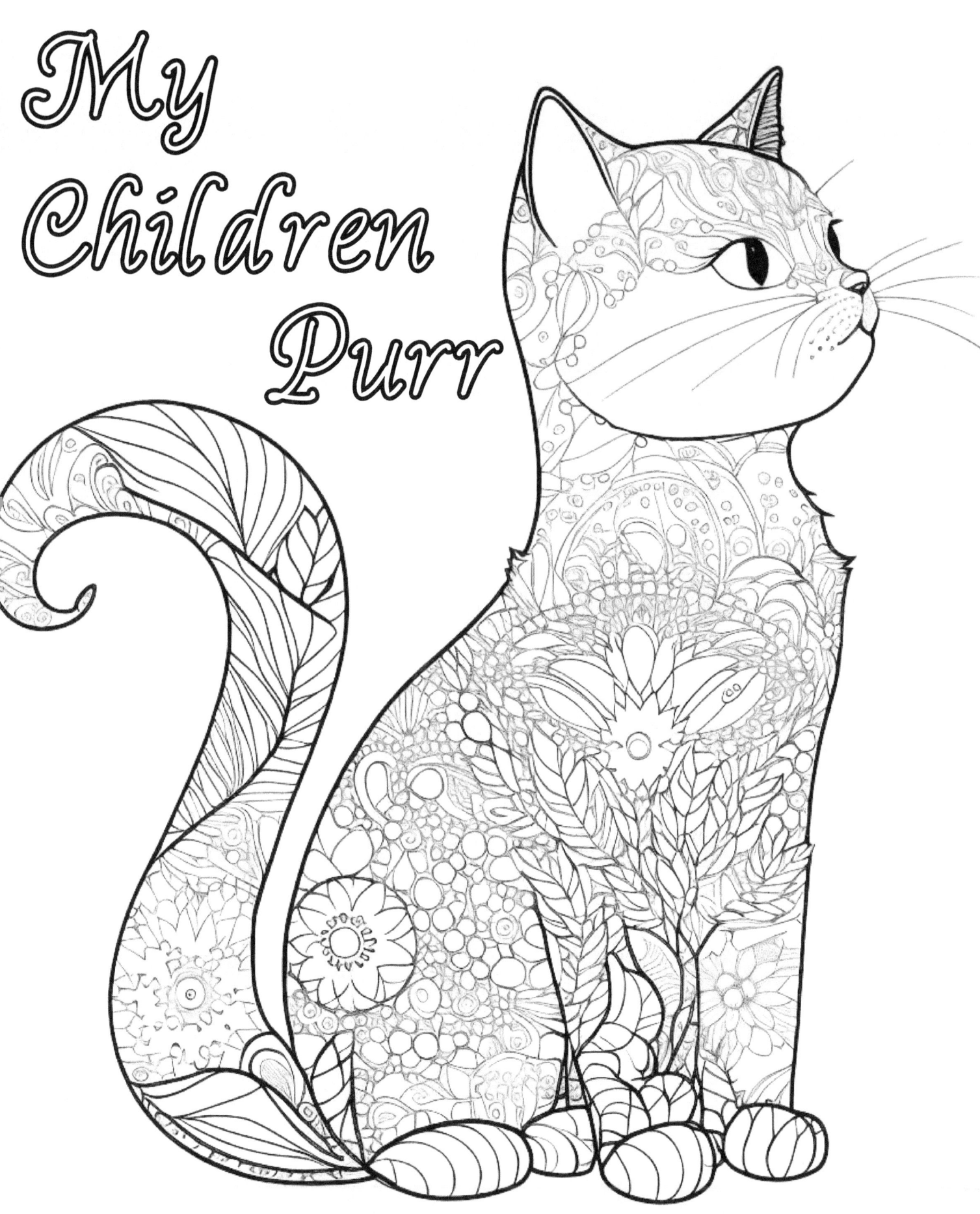

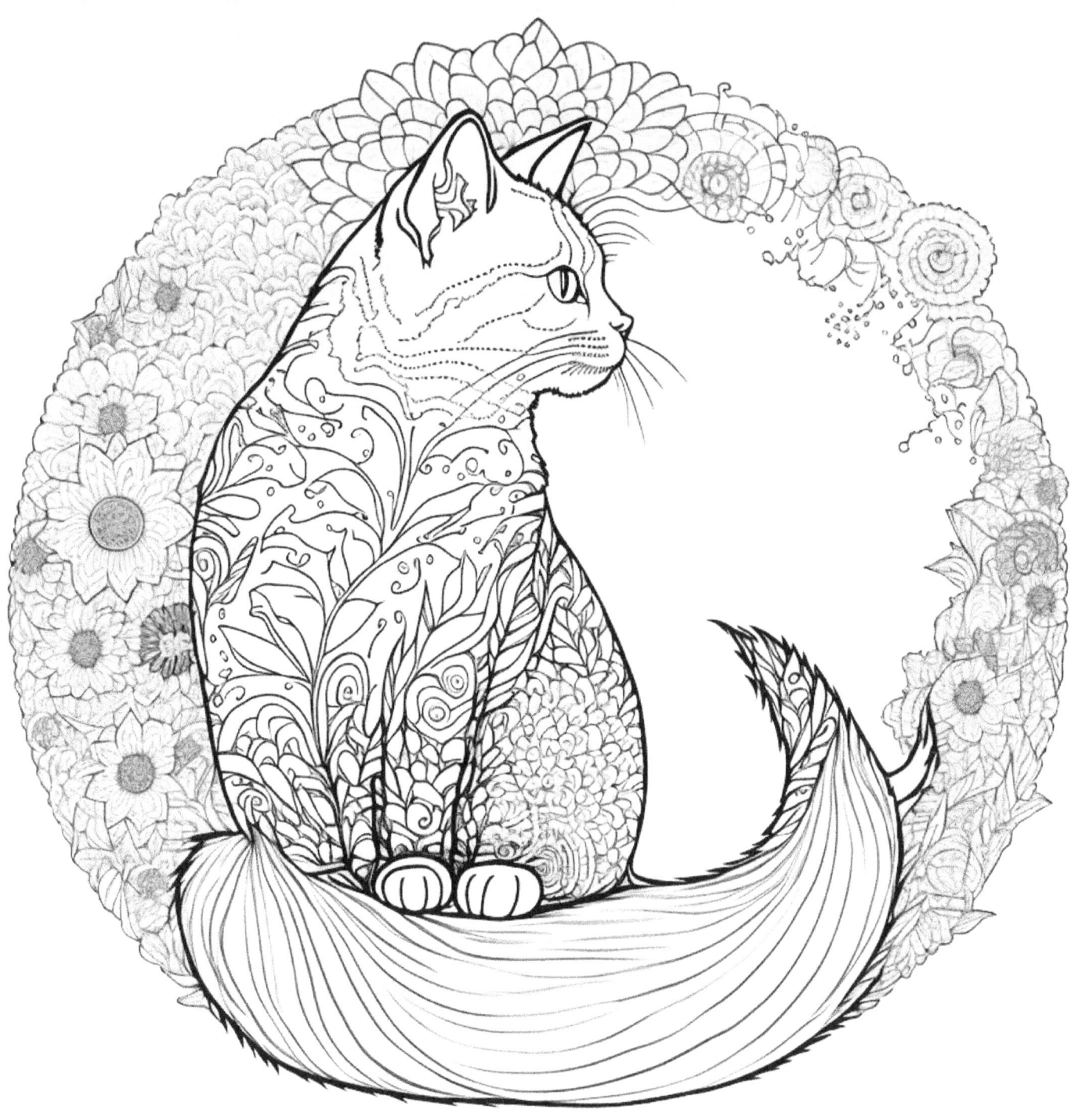

I Just Want To Pet

All The Cats

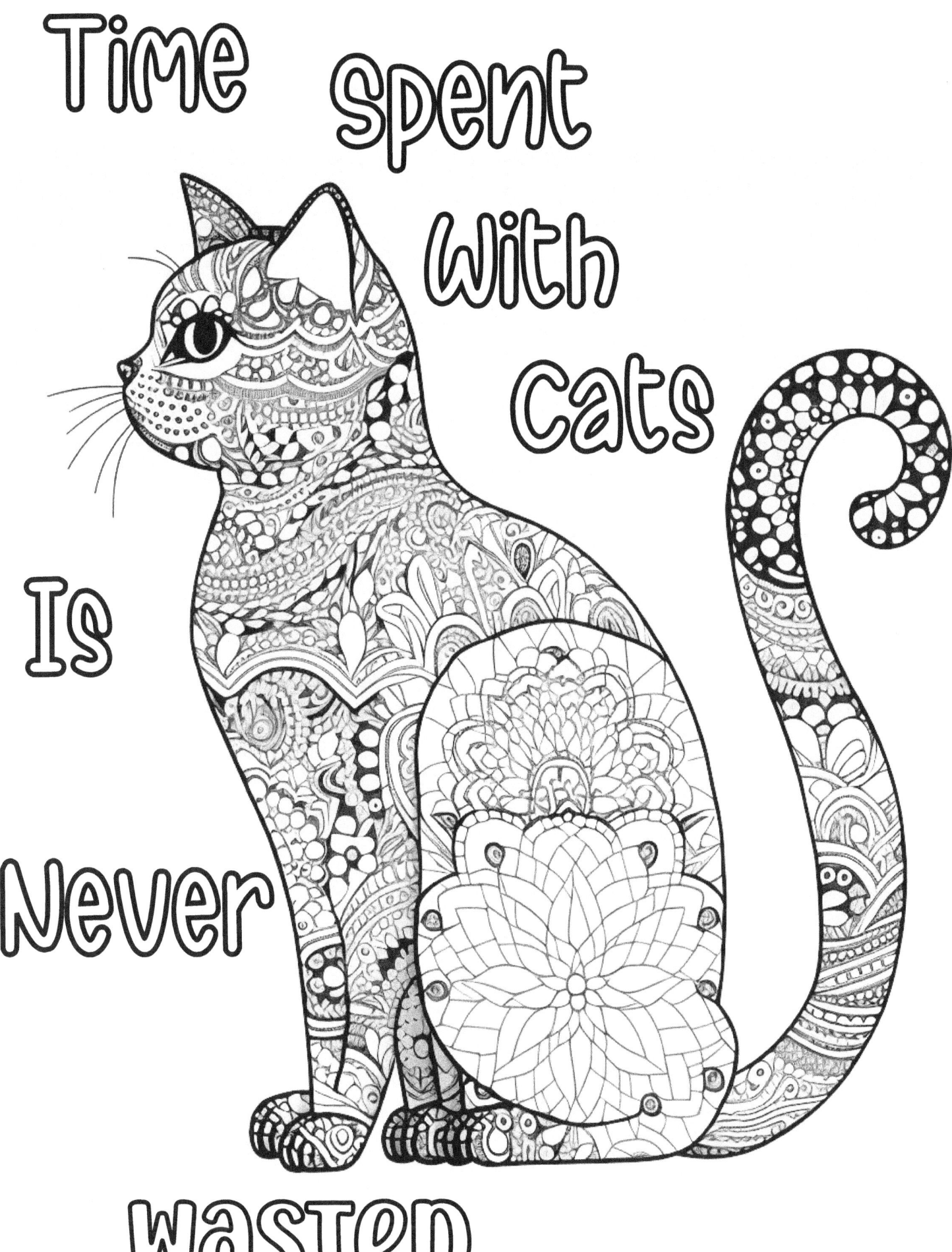

THE SMALLEST
Feline
IS A
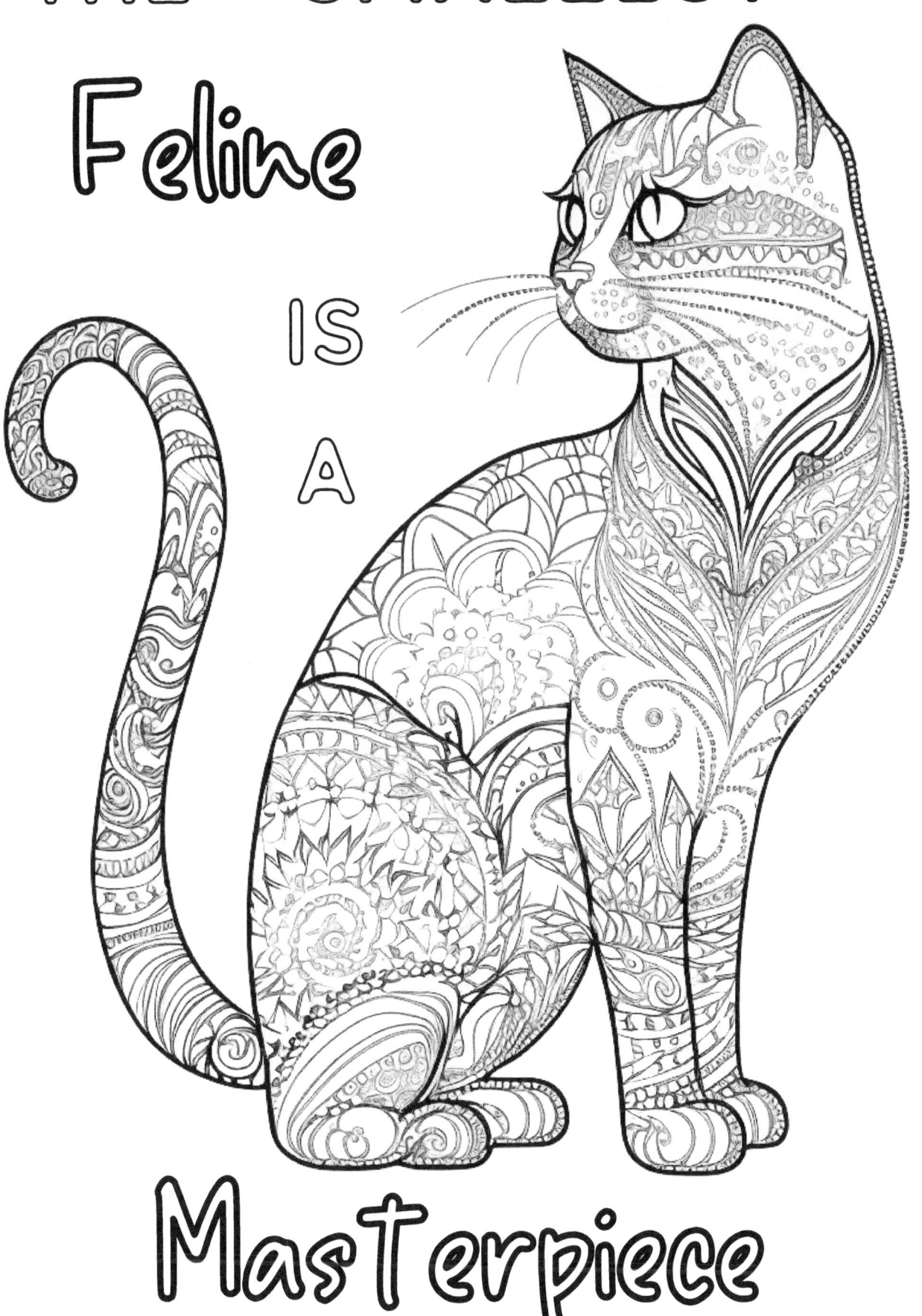
Masterpiece

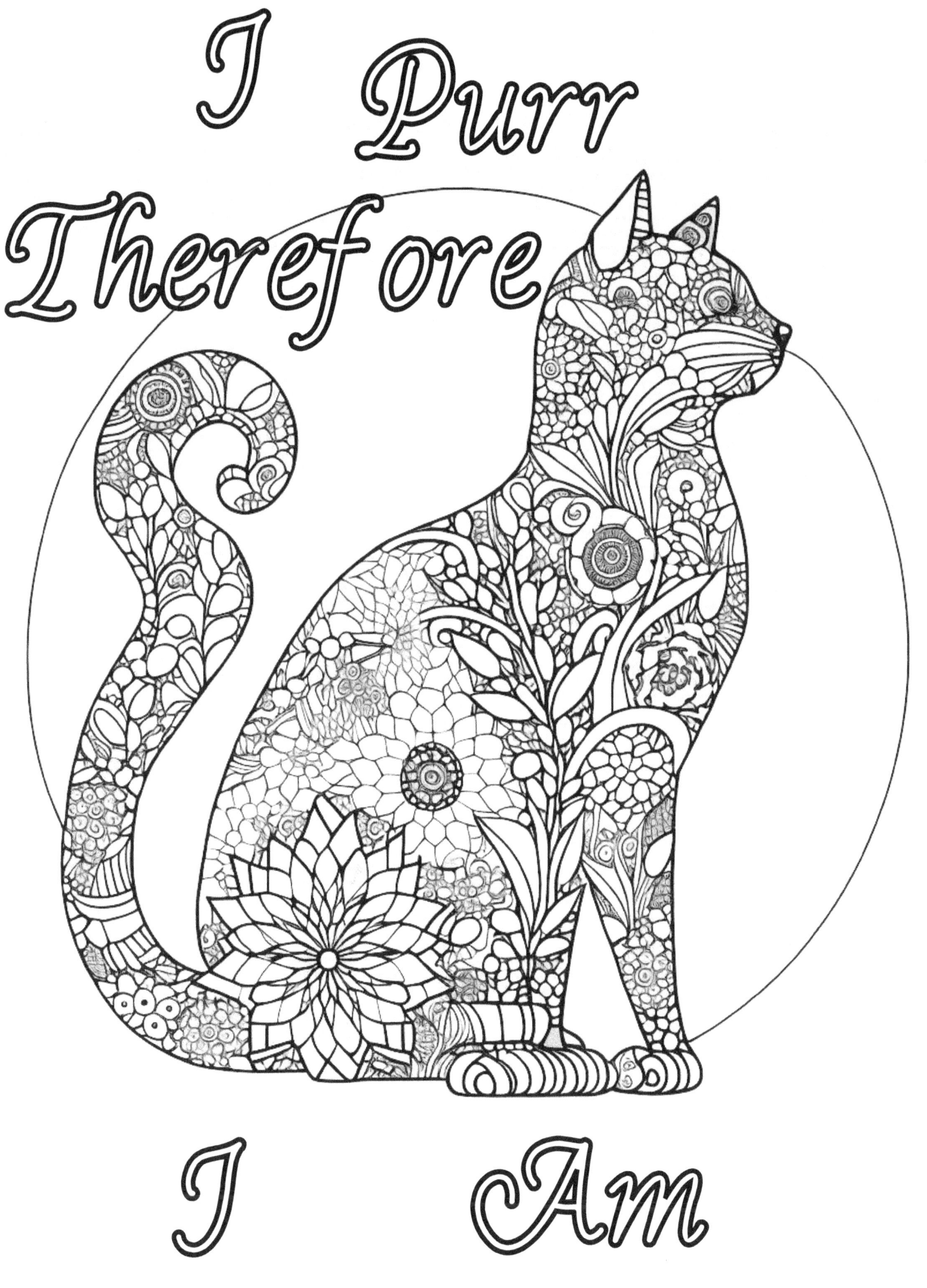

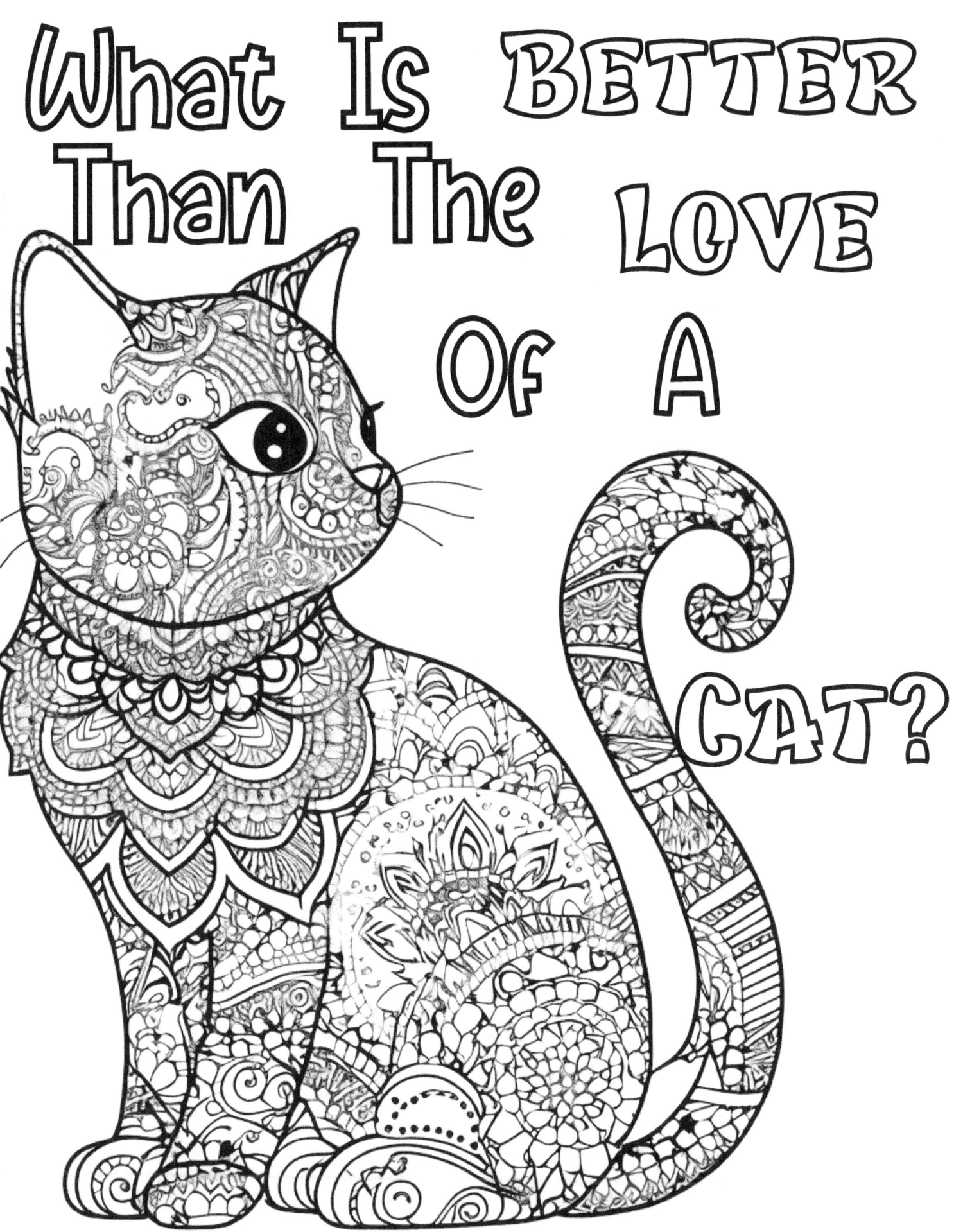

Those Who Love Cats Have Big Hearts

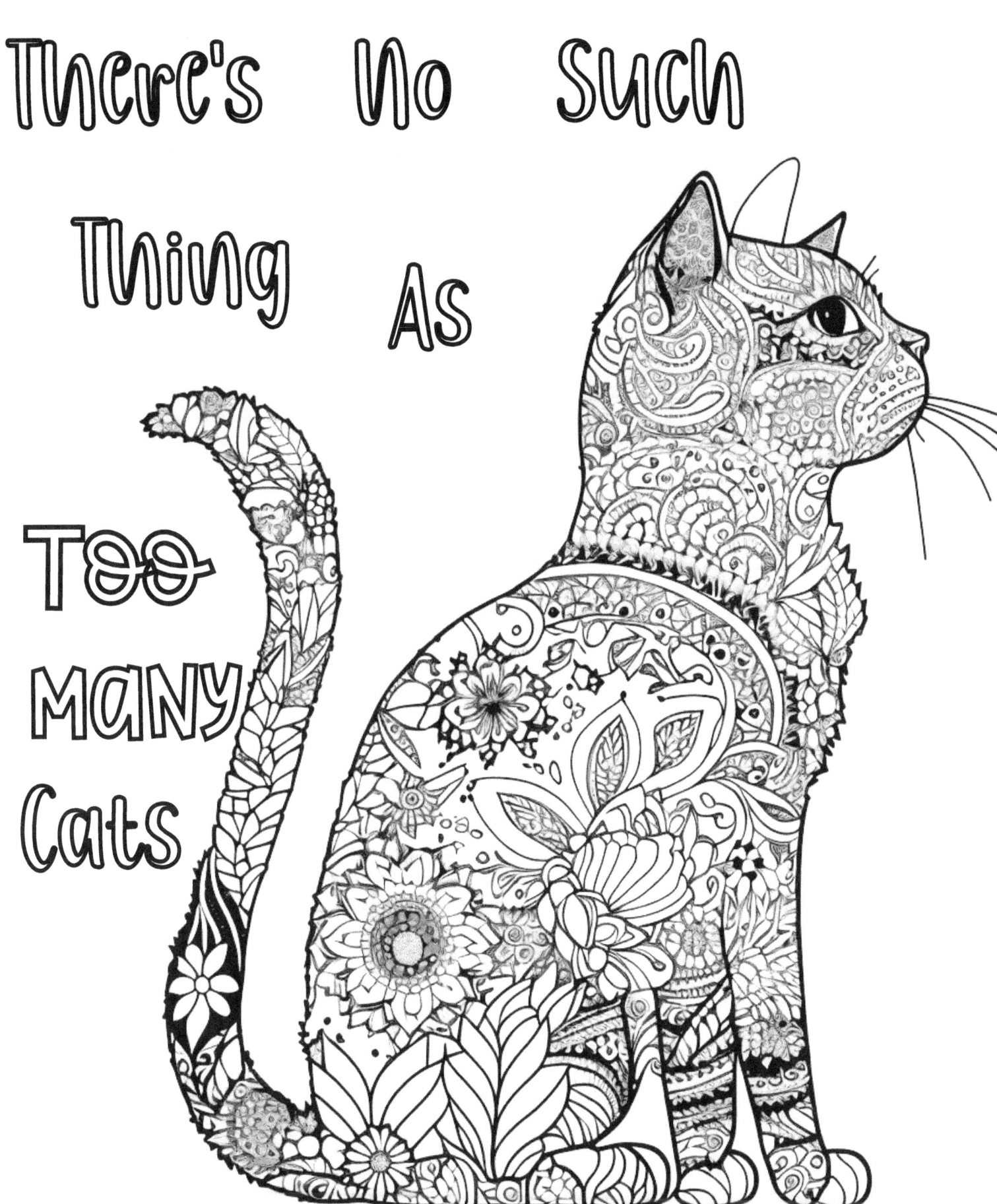

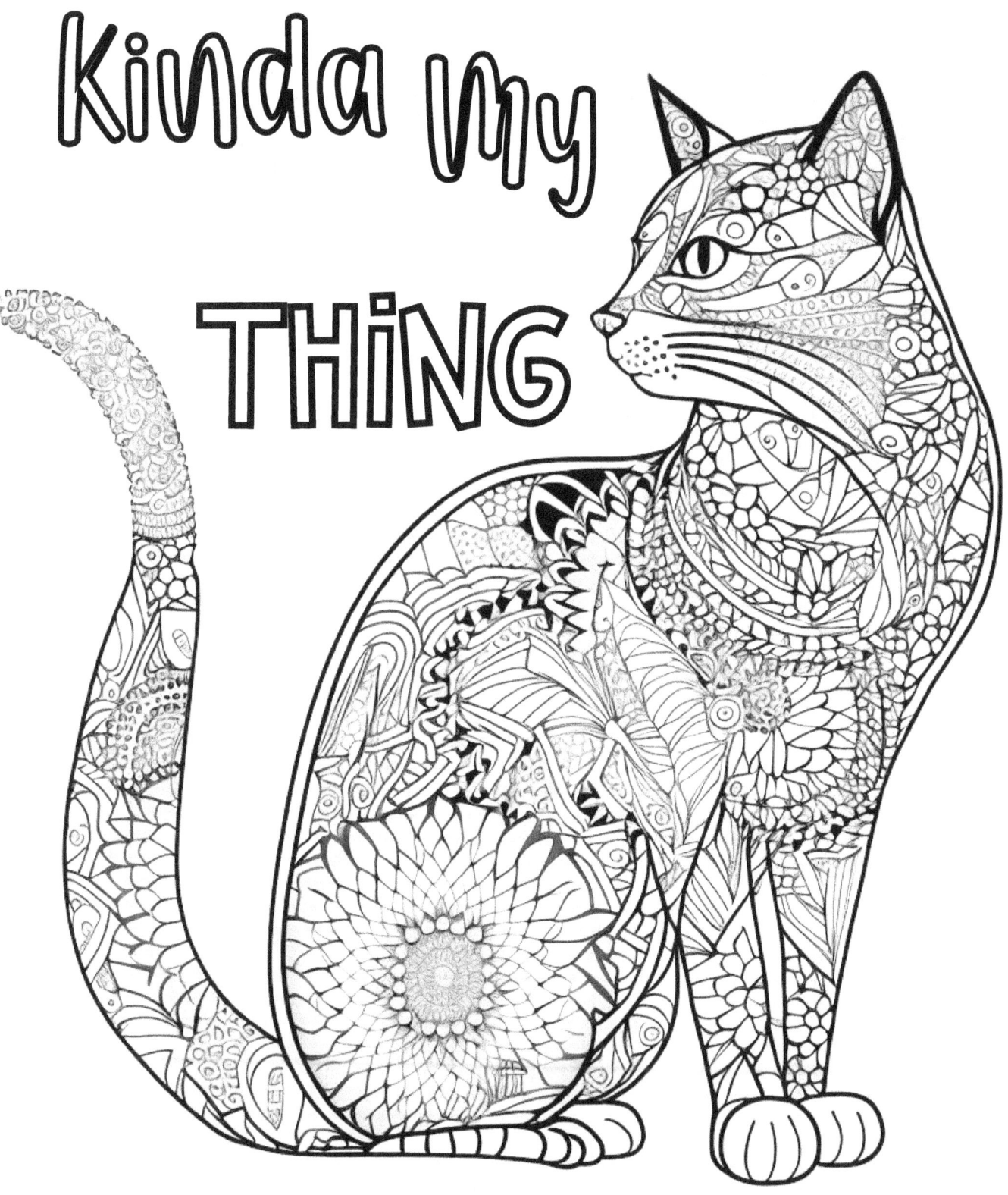

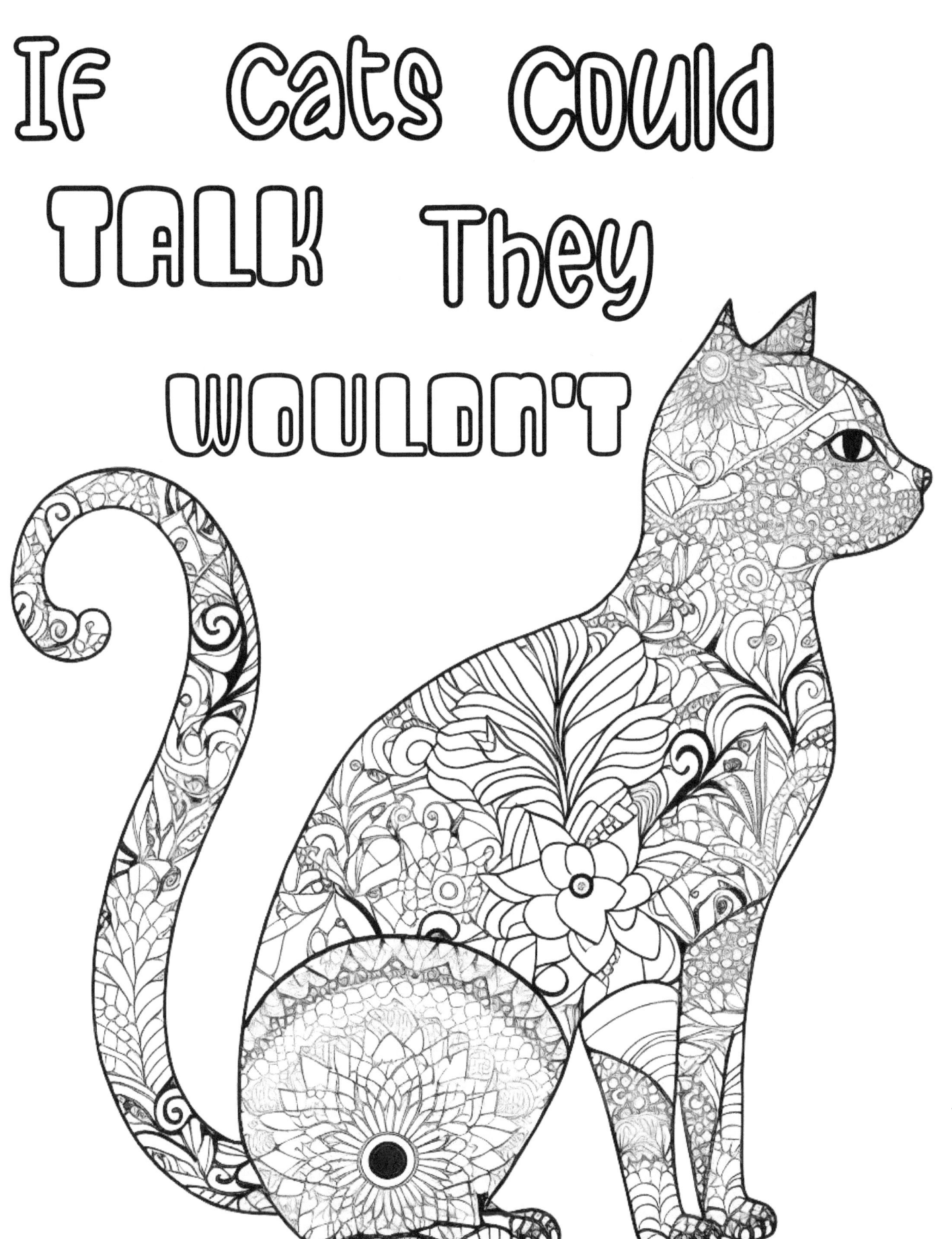

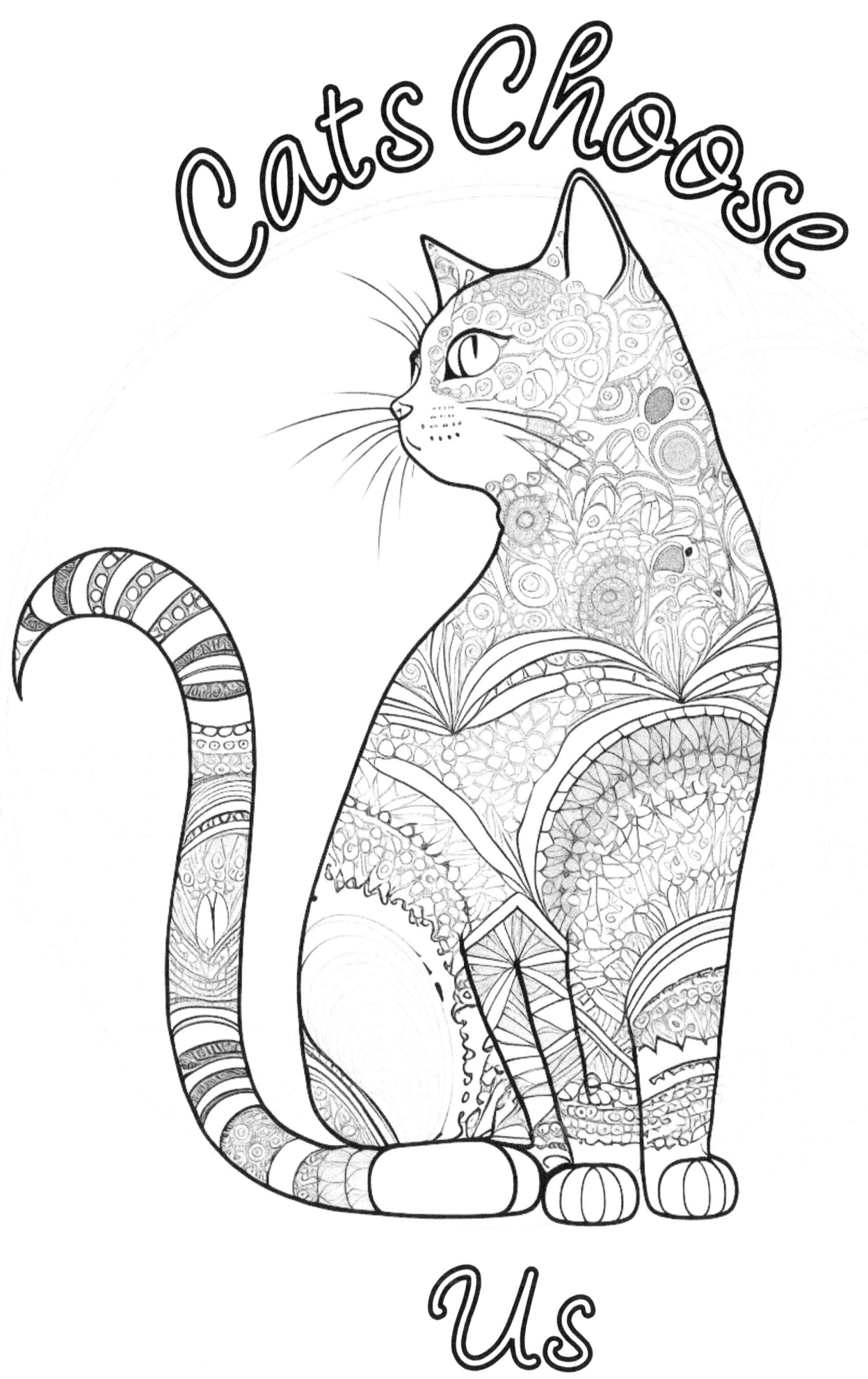

CatS ARE Angels WitH

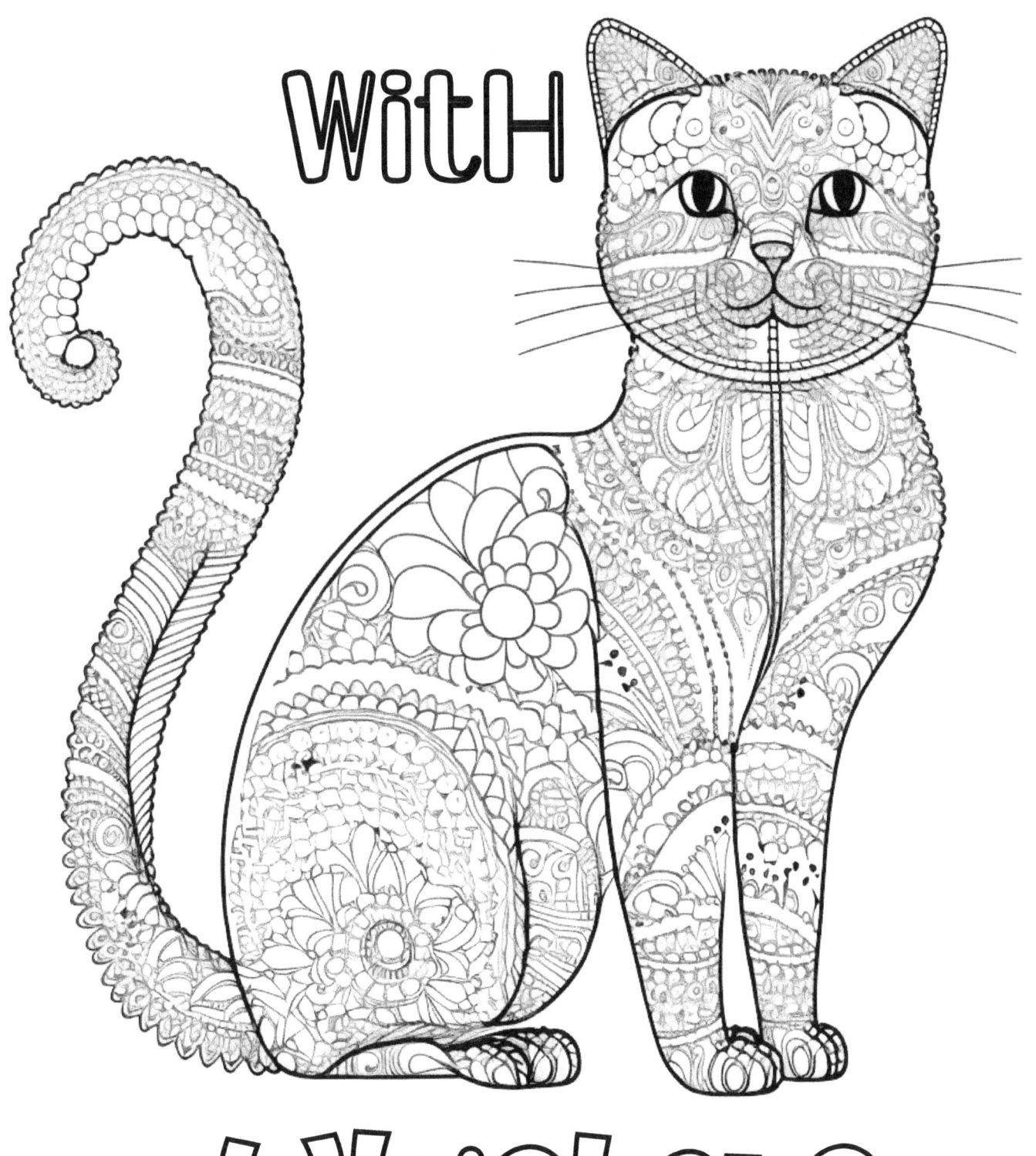

Whiskers

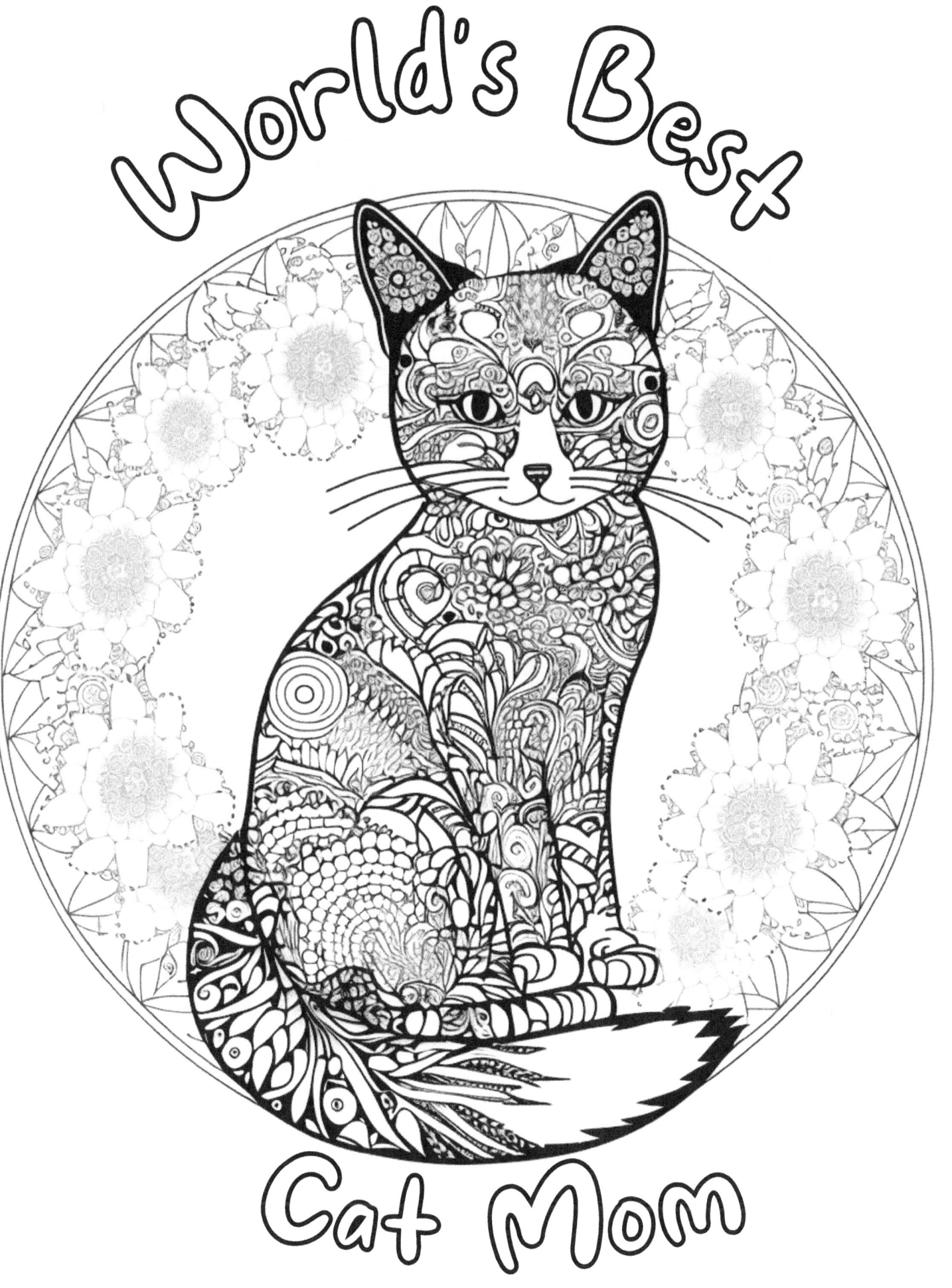

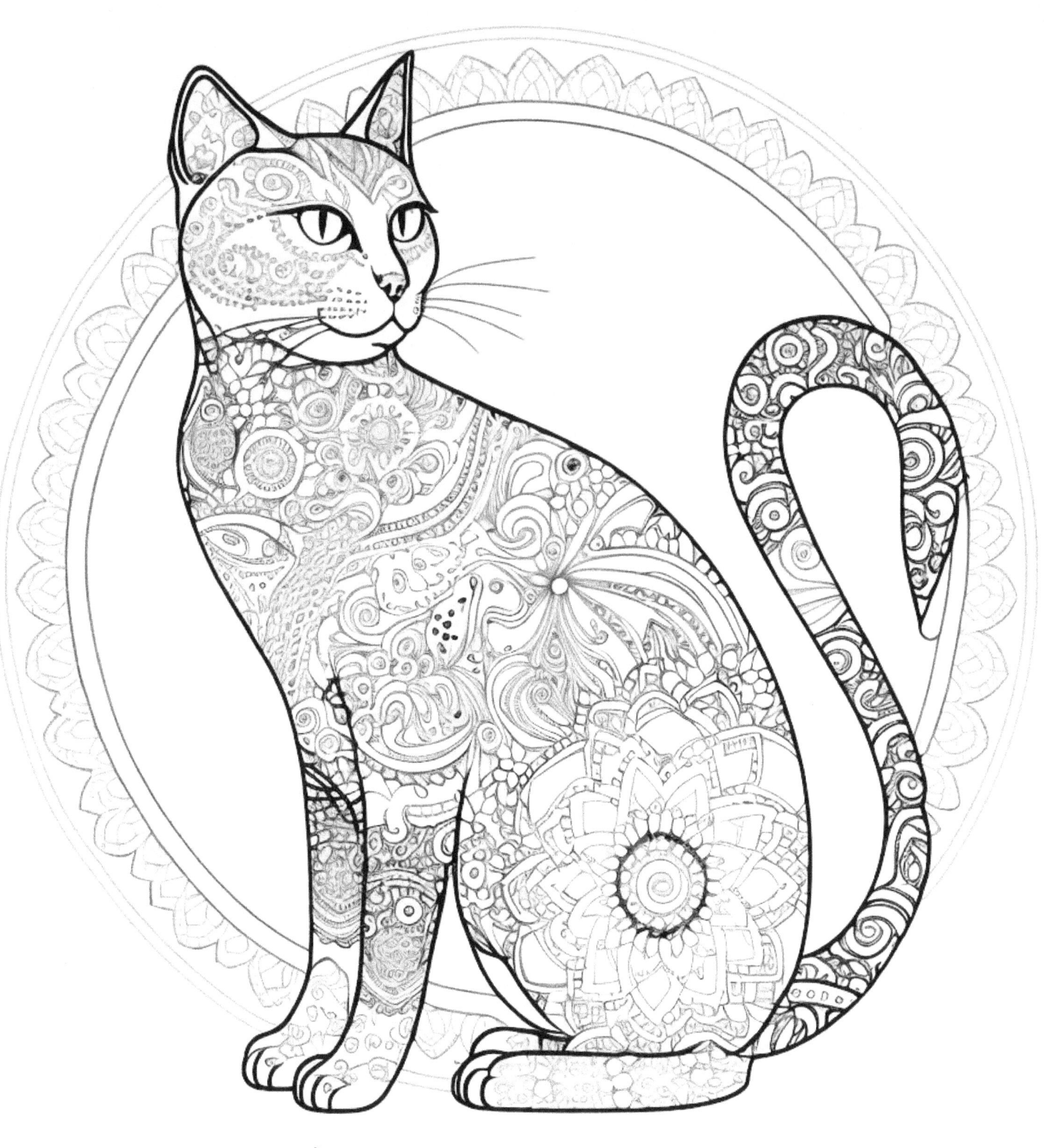

www.ingramcontent.com/pod-product-compliance
Lightning Source LLC
Chambersburg PA
CBHW082153230526

45467CB00044B/3209